My First Team

ICE HOCKEY

by BERNARD CONAGHAN

TABLE OF CONTENTS

A Pelican Book

SEAHORSE PUBLISHING

Teaching Tips for Caregivers and Teachers:

Research shows that one of the best ways for students to learn a new topic is to read about it.

Before Reading

- Read the title and predict what the book will be about.
- Read the "Words to Know" and discuss the meaning of each word.
- Read the back cover to see what the book is about.

During Reading

- When a student gets to a word that is unknown, ask them to look at the rest of the sentence to find clues to help with the meaning of the unknown word.
- Motivate students with praise and encouragement.

After Reading

- Discuss the main idea of the book.
- Ask students to give one detail that they learned in the book.

SIGHT WORDS

a	move	use
an	on	we
are	play	
have	the	

WORDS TO KNOW

goalie

ice hockey

puck

skate

sticks

team

We play **ice hockey**.

ice
hockey

We **skate** on the ice.

skate

stick

We use hockey **sticks**.

We move the **puck** on the ice.

puck

We have a **goalie**.

goalie

We are an ice hockey **team**!

team
12

Index

Written by: Bernard Conaghan
Series Development: James Earley

Photos: Shutterstock

Library of Congress PCN Data
Ice Hockey / Bernard Conaghan
My First Team
ISBN 979-8-8945-9253-4 (hard cover)
ISBN 979-8-8945-9267-1 (paperback)
ISBN 979-8-8945-9295-4 (EPUB)
ISBN 979-8-8945-9281-7 (eBook)
ISBN 979-8-8945-9309-8 (audio)
ISBN 979-8-8945-9323-4 (Read-Along)
Library of Congress Control Number:
2024946356

Printed in Canada/012025/CP20250101

Seahorse Publishing Company
www.seahorsepub.com

Published in the United States
Seahorse Publishing
PO Box 771325
Coral Springs, FL 33077

SEAHORSE PUBLISHING